WATER

© Aladdin Books Ltd

Designed and produced by
Aladdin Books Ltd
70 Old Compton St
London W1

*First published in the
United States 1985 by*
Gloucester Press
387 Park Avenue South
New York, 10016

ISBN 0531 034895

Printed in Belgium

Photographic credits:
Cover and pages 24 and 25, Zefa; pages 8, 10,
13, 14, 19, 20 and 22, Robert Harding; page
17, CEGB.

The cover picture shows the Jackson Dam in
Wyoming, USA.

WATER

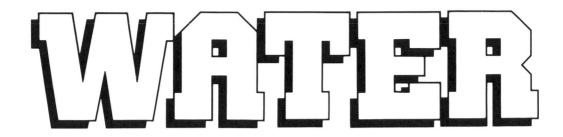

JOHN SATCHWELL

Illustrated by
Ron Hayward Associates

Consultant
Stuart Boyle

Gloucester Press
New York : Toronto

Introduction

It is easy to forget how important energy is to us all. We need it for heating and lighting our houses, schools and offices and for fueling our cars, trains and aircraft. Industries need energy to make their products. This book looks at ways of getting energy from water.

Many sources of energy, such as coal and oil, can only be used once. Eventually the world will run out of them. But the energy we get from rivers and tides will last forever. There will always be water for us to use.

Natural power in a waterfall in Brazil

Contents

Energy from water

The diagram on the opposite page shows how much the different energy sources contribute to the energy we use. In the case of water, this energy is in the form of electricity generated at hydroelectric power stations.

The most usual way of harnessing water power is to build a dam across a river. The water behind the dam can be controlled to generate electricity and also to irrigate nearby farmland. Building a dam is an expensive job which takes many years to complete.

Glen Canyon Dam, USA, took eight years to build

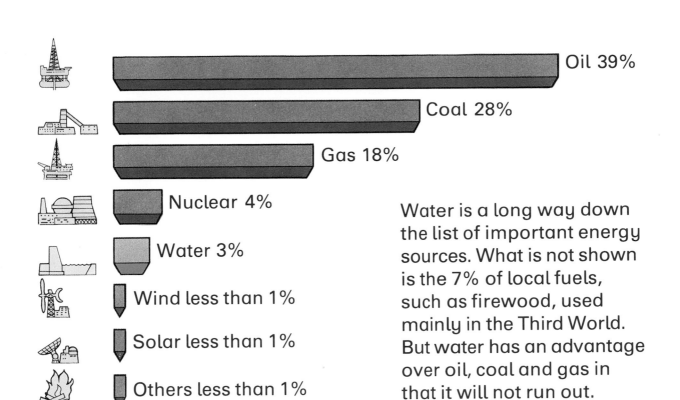

Oil 39%

Coal 28%

Gas 18%

Nuclear 4%

Water 3%

Wind less than 1%

Solar less than 1%

Others less than 1%

Water is a long way down the list of important energy sources. What is not shown is the 7% of local fuels, such as firewood, used mainly in the Third World. But water has an advantage over oil, coal and gas in that it will not run out.

11

Building a dam

A dam must be very strong to withstand the force of the water pressing against it. Some dams are made of concrete, others of clay, earth and gravel.

At the side of the dam is a spillway – a concrete channel down which any floodwater can escape. There are also sluice gates through which a controlled amount of water can be let through. The water flowing through the sluice gates is used to generate electricity. A big dam can provide enough electricity for an entire city.

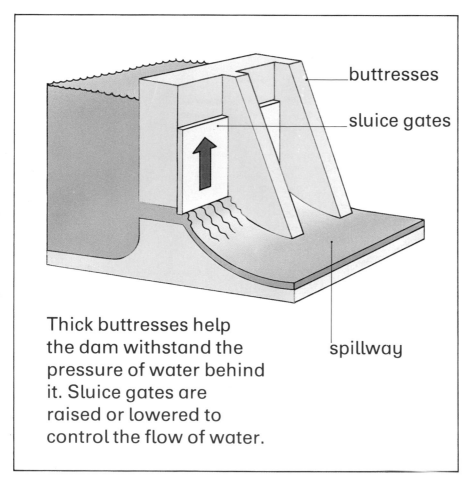

buttresses

sluice gates

spillway

Thick buttresses help the dam withstand the pressure of water behind it. Sluice gates are raised or lowered to control the flow of water.

Tobela Dam, Pakistan

Electricity from water

The rushing water from the dam spins the blades of huge machines called turbines. Each turbine is connected to a generator by a shaft.

Inside the generators are magnets surrounded by thousands of coils of wire. When these magnets are spun by the turbines, they generate electricity in the wire coils. This electricity is carried away in cables.

The turbine room in a hydroelectric power station

Inside the power station the only sound
heard is the steady hum of the spinning
turbines. Everything is spotlessly clean.
The engineers keep a careful watch on the
equipment from their control room.

In modern power stations, computers
automatically switch extra turbines into action
when the demand for electricity is highest.

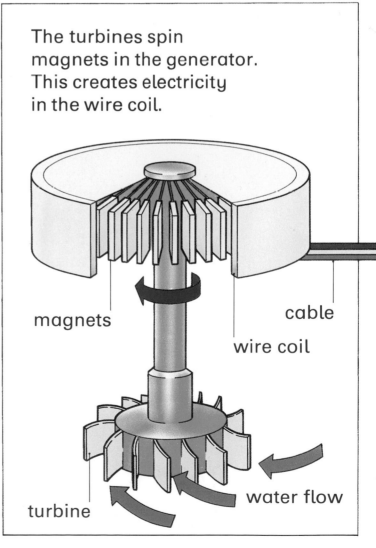

The turbines spin
magnets in the generator.
This creates electricity
in the wire coil.

magnets

cable

wire coil

turbine

water flow

Storing energy

The water in this hydroelectric scheme in a beautiful Welsh valley runs down tunnels blasted out of the inside of the mountain. These tunnels are the biggest man-made caverns in Europe.

The water that has already been used to power the generators collects in a lake at the bottom of the dam. Then, when the demand for electricity is lowest, usually at night, some of the turbines work backward to act as pumps. They pump the water from the lower lake back to the top lake behind the dam, so that it can be used again. This two-way system is called a "pumped storage" system.

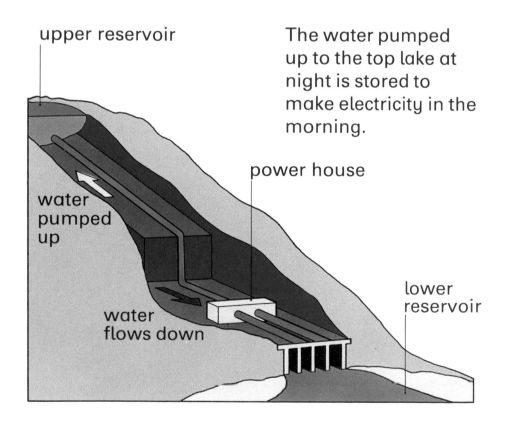

upper reservoir

The water pumped up to the top lake at night is stored to make electricity in the morning.

power house

water pumped up

water flows down

lower reservoir

The Dinorwic scheme, Wales, UK

Using the tides

The ocean has energy which can be harnessed too. This power station makes use of the changing tides. Built across an estuary, it shuts in the water from the high tide. As the tide rises, the water flows through the barrier and collects in the estuary. As it does so, it drives turbines to generate electricity.

Rance tidal power station in Brittany, France

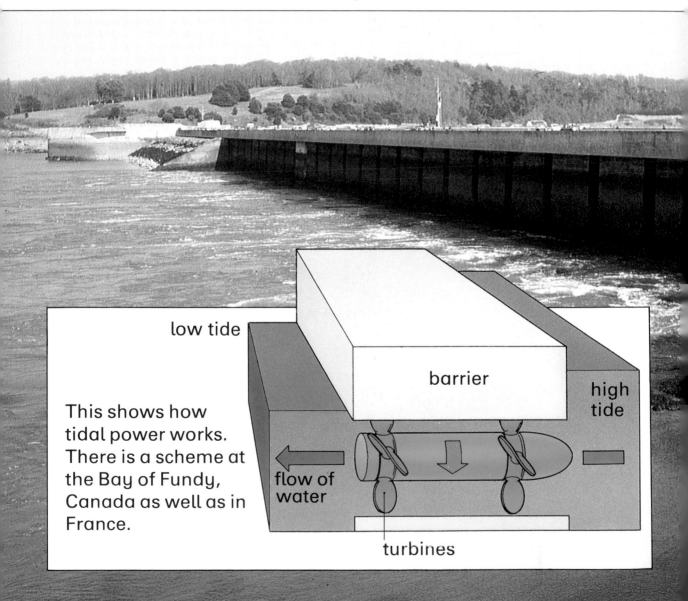

low tide

barrier

high tide

This shows how tidal power works. There is a scheme at the Bay of Fundy, Canada as well as in France.

flow of water

turbines

When the tide drops, water trapped in the estuary is allowed to flow back to the sea. Once again, the water turns the turbines that are built to generate electricity no matter which way the water flows.

In the future, the energy of ocean waves may also be tamed.

Natural heat

Steam drives the turbines at this power station in New Zealand. How is the water heated? In a few parts of the world hot water springs naturally from the ground. In these places there are cracks in the Earth's crust, where the heat at the Earth's core can escape.

Geothermal power plant at Wairakei, New Zealand

The energy obtained from hot water and steam from beneath the Earth is called geothermal power.

In Reykjavik, in Iceland, houses are heated by water from hot springs. It can be used to generate electricity too.

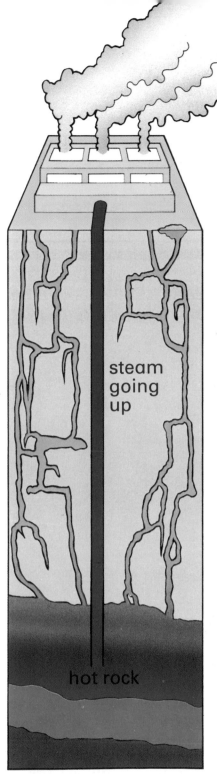

steam going up

hot rock

In a geothermal power station, a hole is often drilled deep underground to channel steam to the power station.

Cooling towers at a power station

Water in industry

All sorts of industries rely on water. At the coal-fueled power station shown here, millions of liters are used every day. The water is boiled to make steam to drive turbines, and so produce electricity. More water is needed to cool this steam down again, so that it can be fed back to the boilers.

Cooling and cleaning are probably the two most important uses for water in industry. Other products actually contain water – paper and many chemicals, for example, as well as canned food and drinks.

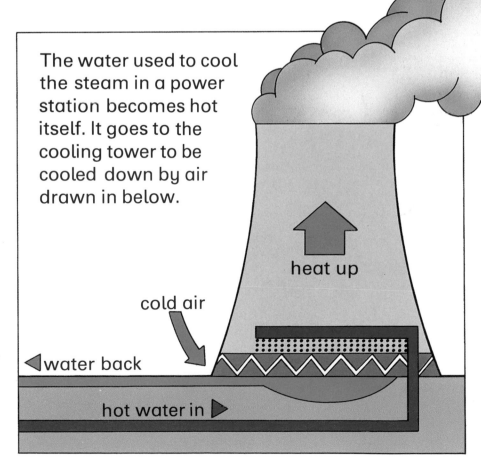

The water used to cool the steam in a power station becomes hot itself. It goes to the cooling tower to be cooled down by air drawn in below.

heat up

cold air

◁ water back

hot water in ▷

Water to your home

Water is available at the turn of a tap for many of us. But it might have to travel a long way before it reaches our homes.

Water from rivers, lakes and wells is collected in large reservoirs. When it has been filtered and made fit to drink it flows on to a covered reservoir. From there it is pumped along pipes to all the places that need it. The pipes are underground. They run underneath your road and into your house.

You heat water for hot drinks, baths, laundry and heating. You also use it to help plants grow – and to keep cool!

One everyday use for water!

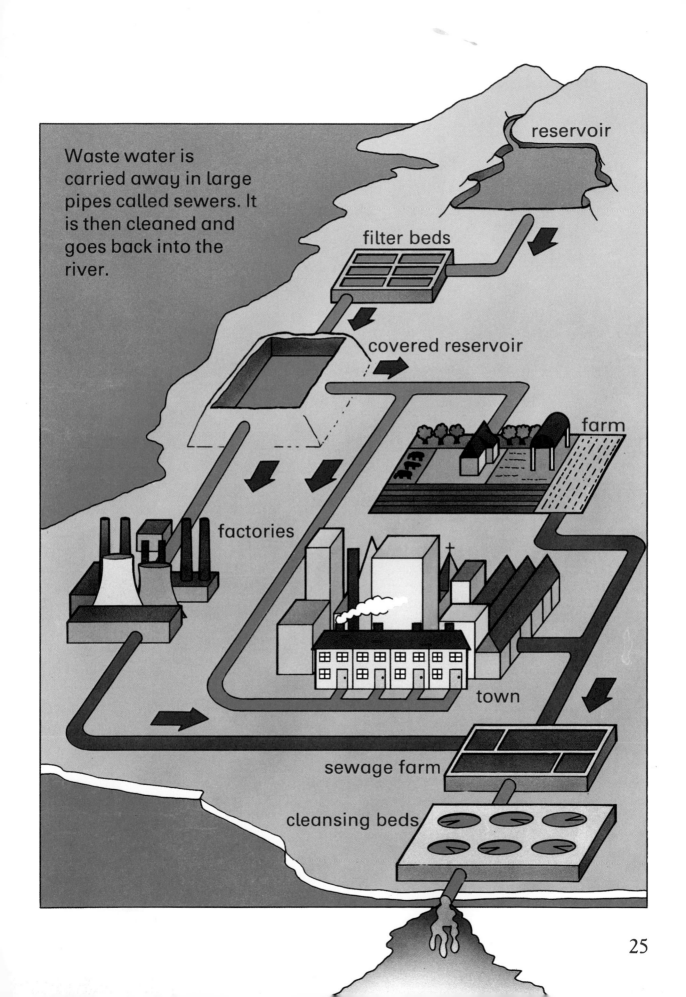

Waste water is carried away in large pipes called sewers. It is then cleaned and goes back into the river.

reservoir

filter beds

covered reservoir

farm

factories

town

sewage farm

cleansing beds

Irrigation and wells

Many parts of the world do not have regular rainfall. Crops grown in this place in Brazil used to be ruined by floods twice a year. Dams built across the rivers have controlled the water.

In other regions there is not enough water to grow food. Water from nearby rivers and lakes can be taken to where it's needed by pipelines and channels. This is called irrigation. The irrigation channels need constant maintenance to keep them from being blocked.

Water is often trapped underground between layers of hard rock. In many dry regions, bores or wells are dug to bring this water to the surface so that people can use it.

Water trapped in a layer of underground rock is brought to the surface by digging a well.

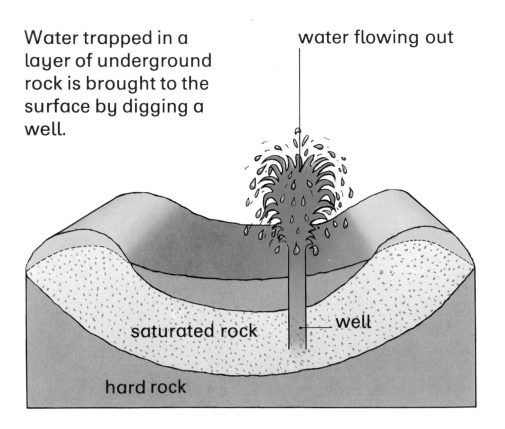

water flowing out

saturated rock

well

hard rock

Tending irrigation ditches on a Brazilian plantation

Fact file 1

Using the muscle power of animals was probably our first step in harnessing energy. Animals are strong, but do get tired. The flow of water is stronger, and never tires.

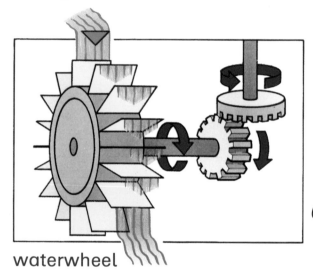

waterwheel

Water can push the blades of a waterwheel with enormous force. This rotation was first used to turn millstones which ground corn. Later, they were used to blow air into furnaces to help make iron. The turbines shown on page 15 are simply modern versions of the waterwheel.

Steam engines finally replaced the water wheel in industry, but some can be found today. Most villages and towns had a mill, so you may be able to find one if you look hard enough.

Power from water is useful, but water for growing food is even more important. Irrigation is the supply of river or lake water through channels to places where the rainfall is poor.

The bucket is the oldest invention for lifting water up from a river, but this is very tiring. The Egyptians still use a bucket with a counterweight called a shaduf, which makes the lifting easier.

Archimedes' screw

But the Greeks invented a better method than the Egyptians called the Archimedes' screw. This is a spiral or screw enclosed in a cylinder. By turning a handle water could be drawn up from the river. This is still used in some parts of the world.

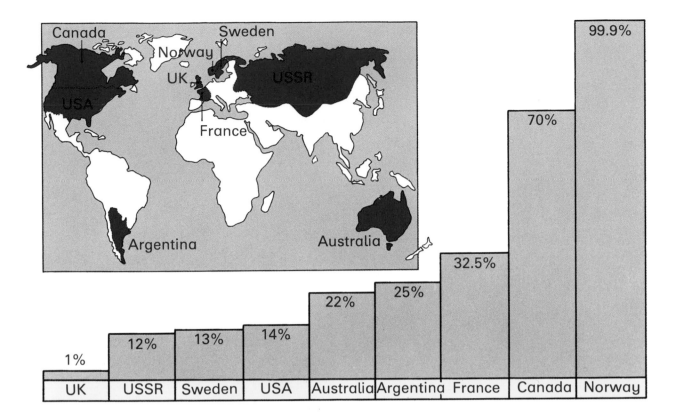

The diagram above shows how much hydroelectricity is produced by some countries. The figure is in relation to the total amount of electricity made from all sources.

Hydroelectricity is most used in countries that have many fast-flowing rivers. If countries also have cheap supplies of coal and oil, then electricity is often made by burning these fuels and water power may be neglected.

Norway has a small population and plenty of fast-flowing rivers. This makes it possible to make all its electricity from water.

For some time the USSR has thought about actually changing the course of huge rivers to carry water south from Siberia. This scheme would make a new "lake" the size of Italy!

The UK, at the other end of the diagram, could not make all the electricity it needs from water. But with large reserves of coal, water power is less important.

Most other countries shown are making serious attempts to exploit hydroelectricity. Fuels such as oil and gas may only last for another 100 years, while water power will last forever.

Fact file 2

There are various kinds of dam. Each one is suited to the geography of its area and materials available. The simplest is the Gravity dam that resists the push of the water by its weight. It has a central waterproof core.

Buttress dams are similar in shape to gravity dams. They are used when the site demands a long, straight dam. The buttresses behind the dam face prevent the water pushing the dam head over heels.

gravity dam

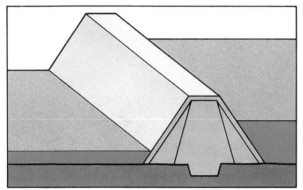

buttress dam

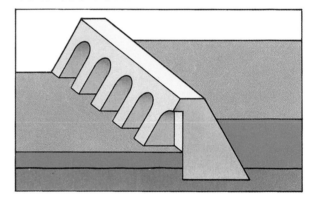

Arch dams are built on rivers with high banks and across steep-sided gorges. The push of the water would normally straighten out the arch, but this is resisted by the river bank.

Cantilever dams are thin concrete walls. They manage to resist the push of the water by having metal rods bedded into the wall. They are often called reinforced dams.

arch dam

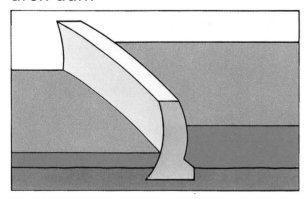

cantilever dam

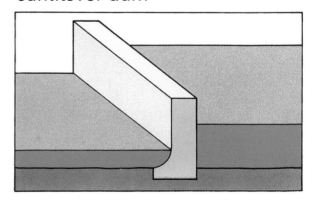

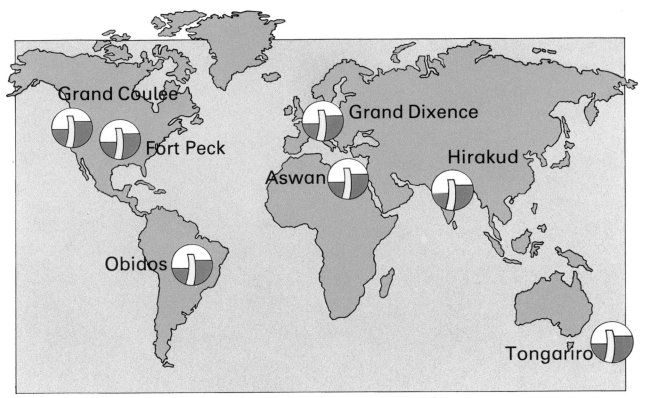

Some dams and irrigation schemes of the world

Schemes for electricity and irrigation from water are only worth having if the river is big enough. Most countries in the world have at least one river where dam projects are worthwhile.

The largest concrete dam in the world is the Grand Coulee Dam on the Columbia river in USA. It took ten years to build.

The longest river dam in the world is the Hirakud in India.

New Zealand gets 70% of its electricity from water power. The main contribution is from the Tongariro project.

Grand Dixence in Switzerland is the highest dam in the world. It is 285 meters (935 feet) high.

Fort Peck on the Missouri river in America contains the largest volume of material. Finished in 1940, it contains nearly a million cubic meters (35 million cubic feet) of earth and rock.

The Aswan Dam in Egypt was built on the Nile river to both make electricity and irrigate land.

Brazil has plans to dam the mighty Amazon river at Obidos. The lake created behind the dam will have an area of 177,100 square km (68,400 square miles).

Fact file 3

The total amount of water in the world is 1.5 billion cubic km (0.5 billion cubic miles). Most of this is the saltwater of oceans and seas and cannot be used for drinking.

About 2% of the world's water supply is locked up in glaciers and in the ice caps of the North and South Poles. In the future, ways may be found to make use of some this vast reserve of potential water power.

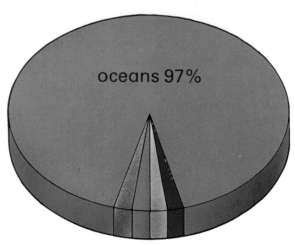

The world's water supply

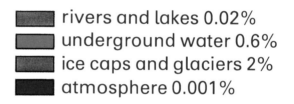

rivers and lakes 0.02%
underground water 0.6%
ice caps and glaciers 2%
atmosphere 0.001%

The diagram below shows how much water is needed to produce even the simple everyday articles that we in the Western world take for granted. On food alone, for an average daily diet, the water required for production, packaging and transport is 33,000 liters (8,719 gallons) per person.

Enormous amounts are used in industry. Some 450,000 liters (118,900 gallons) of water are used to make one car, for example. It is used for washing, cooling, and it may be part of the end product. Soft drinks are almost all water.

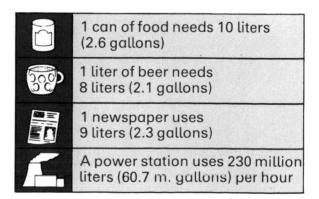

An egg needs 1,000 liters (264 gallons).	1 can of food needs 10 liters (2.6 gallons)
1 kilo (2.2 lbs) of sugar needs 8,000 liters (2,114 gallons).	1 liter of beer needs 8 liters (2.1 gallons)
1 liter of milk needs 140 liters (37 gallons)	1 newspaper uses 9 liters (2.3 gallons)
1 kilo of rice needs 4,500 liters (1,190 gallons)	A power station uses 230 million liters (60.7 m. gallons) per hour

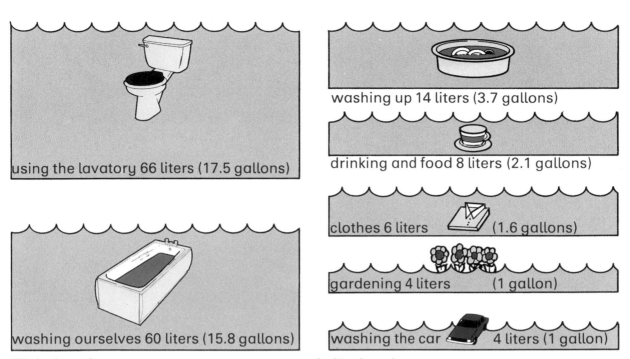

using the lavatory 66 liters (17.5 gallons)

washing up 14 liters (3.7 gallons)

drinking and food 8 liters (2.1 gallons)

clothes 6 liters (1.6 gallons)

gardening 4 liters (1 gallon)

washing ourselves 60 liters (15.8 gallons)

washing the car 4 liters (1 gallon)

This is where our water goes on a daily basis

Water is essential for life. It is possible to live without shelter and even without clothes, but without water life would end in a few days. The minimum of drinking water is about one liter per day (0.2 gallons).

In a modern city, the average water consumption may be as much as 1,800 liters (475 gallons) per person. If the population of that city is a million people, then the pumps, pipes and purification systems must be very large indeed. After use, that water must be carried away by more pipes and pumps to be cleaned for reuse.

Shortage of water is not a problem of amount. The flow of a single large river such as the Yangtze in China could supply all of the people of the world with 680 liters (180 gallons) per day.

Storing water in places where the rainfall is irregular and distributing river-water over long distances is very expensive. Rich countries can afford to do it and poor ones usually cannot carry out irrigation schemes. Money is the difference between a bath every day and drinking dirty water from a polluted well.

Glossary

Cooling towers Water is often heated up in industrial processes, and needs to be cooled for reuse. This is done by cold air fed into towers. Some steam escapes from the funnels.

Estuary This is where a river runs into the sea. This part of the river contains both salt and fresh water, and the water rises and falls with the tides.

Hot springs These occur when cold water seeps into the Earth's crust on to very hot rocks below.

Ice caps These are vast sheets of frozen water, found around Greenland and the North Pole and in Antarctica.

Pumped storage system A two-way hydroelectric water scheme. Water flows down into the power station to turn the turbines. Then it is pumped up again to be used again.

Sluice gates Giant steel barriers or gates. They can be opened or closed to control the flow of water to a power station.

Turbine A machine that is made to rotate by water or steam pressure.

Index

Acknowledgements
*The publishers wish to thank the following
organisations who have helped in the
preparation of this book:*
Central Electricity Generating Board UK,
Energy Technology Support Unit, Friends of
the Earth, National Water Council UK, North
of Scotland Hydro Board, Thames Water
Authority, UK Department of Energy.

PRINTED IN BELGIUM BY

INTERNATIONAL BOOK PRODUCTION